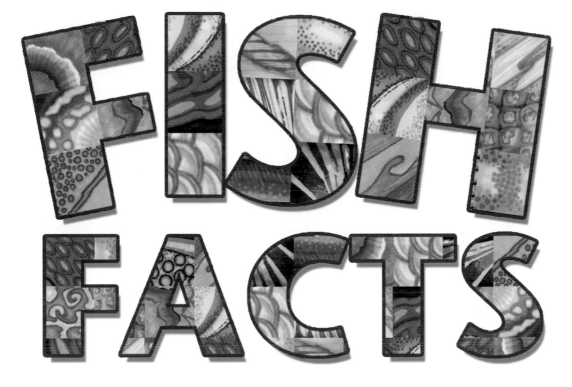

FISH FACTS

By Geoff Swinney
Illustrated by Janeen Mason

Whale Shark

PELICAN PUBLISHING COMPANY

Gretna 2011

For fish heads everywhere especially my Kevins, my brothers, my grandsons, and Ben. —J.M.
In memory of Irene Gernheuser.

First published by the National Museums of Scotland, 1991
Published by arrangement with the National Museums of Scotland
        by Pelican Publishing Company, Inc., 1994
First full-color edition published by Pelican Publishing Company, Inc., 2011

First Pelican edition, 1994
First full-color edition, 2011

The word "Pelican" and the depiction of a pelican are trademarks
of Pelican Publishing Company, Inc., and are registered in the
U.S. Patent and Trademark Office.

Library of Congress Cataloging-in-Publication Data

Swinney, Geoff.
 Fish facts / by Geoff Swinney ; illustrated by Janeen Mason.—1st full-color ed.
    p. cm.
 Includes index.
 ISBN 978-1-58980-908-6 (hardcover : alk. paper) 1. Fishes—Miscellanea. I. Mason, Janeen I. II. Title.
 QL617.S95 2011
 597—dc22
                            2010046220

Heirarchy of Classification

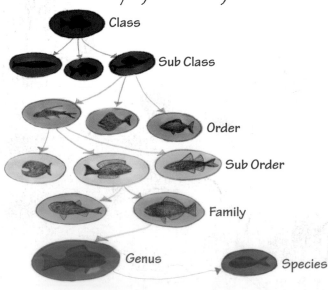

Class

Sub Class

Order

Sub Order

Family

Genus

Species

Printed in Singapore
Published by Pelican Publishing Company, Inc.
1000 Burmaster Street, Gretna, Louisiana 70053

The World of Fish

Viewed from space, Earth is the Blue Planet—over 70 percent of its surface is covered by water. At 4 miles a second, it still takes 25 minutes to cross the Pacific!

Water

"Three-quarters of the world's surface is covered by water."
"Three quarters of the world belongs to the fish."
—David Attenborough

Fish live in nearly all the waters of planet Earth, from high mountain lakes and streams to the bottom of the deepest ocean trenches.

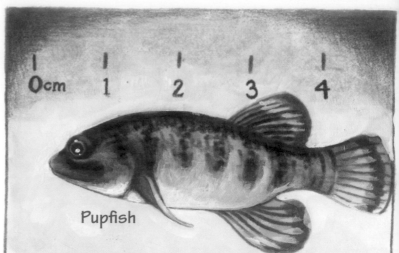

Pupfish

Various pupfish live in North American deserts, some in water up to 44° C.

Icefish

To icy Antarctic seas . . . Icefish contain a special antifreeze which prevents their blood freezing.

Tripod Fish

Highest Lake
Lake Titicaca,
South America

Deepest Ocean
Marina Trench,
Pacific Ocean

From raging torrents . . .

The flattened, disc-like shape of the Bornean Sucker enables it to cling to the rocks of the torrent streams of Borneo.

Bornean Sucker

To the gentle currents near the deep ocean floor.
Tripod fish rest on the sea bed on long, delicate fin rays.

4

More than twenty-one thousand species
of fish live on Earth. Half the known
vertebrate animals alive today are fish.

Ranging in size from huge giants...
The largest fish is the whale shark which may
reach a length of 18 meters or 59 feet.

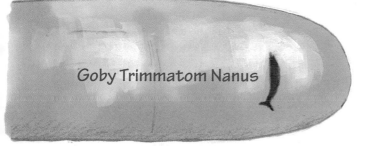

Goby Trimmatom Nanus

... to tiny gobies less than 10 mm in length...
The smallest fish so far discovered is the Goby Trimmatom Nanus
from the Indian and Eastern Pacific oceans.

Cyclothone Microdon

10 mm

Some are very common ... Cyclothone Microdon
is a deep-sea fish found in huge numbers in all the oceans
of the world, except at the poles. It is perhaps the most
common vertebrate on Earth, with populations of billions.

Devil's Hole Pupfish

... Others are very rare.... The Devil's Hole Pupfish lives
naturally nowhere else but in one pool, 18 m long, 3 m wide,
and 90 m deep, in the Nevada desert. The entire population,
which is never more than about eight hundred individuals, lives
on a shallow rock ledge in the pool.

30

20

10
FEET

Lake Sturgeon

Lake Sturgeon can live up to eighty years. There is even one claim of an individual 145 years of age.

Carp

Nobody is very sure how long sharks live, but some species live for seventy years or more, while some others just live a few months.

Carp are also long-lived. Surviving for about fifty years, it's claimed that some individuals of domesticated varieties may live 250 years.

Killifish

Some species of killifish are "annuals"—they live in pools which dry up for part of the year. Annual killifish have evolved to take advantage of the abundant insect food available in the seasonal pools. As pools fill in the wet season, the eggs hatch. Young fish mature quickly and spawn after a few months. The ponds dry up and all adults die, but eggs survive the drought to hatch next wet season.

Freshwater or Salt?

There is ten thousand times more seawater than freshwater on Earth, yet two out of every five species of fish live in freshwater.

This is because these habitats are more varied and because freshwater populations become more easily isolated, by changes in water level, for instance . . .

As the water level of a lake falls, the population can be separated into two new, smaller bodies of water.

The isolated populations may evolve differently in response to different conditions in the two lakes. Long isolation sometimes results in them becoming so different that if they eventually mix again they no longer interbreed—they have become different species.

Most species live either only in seawater or only in freshwater, but a few migrate between the two.

Two of the best known are the Atlantic Salmon and the European Eel.

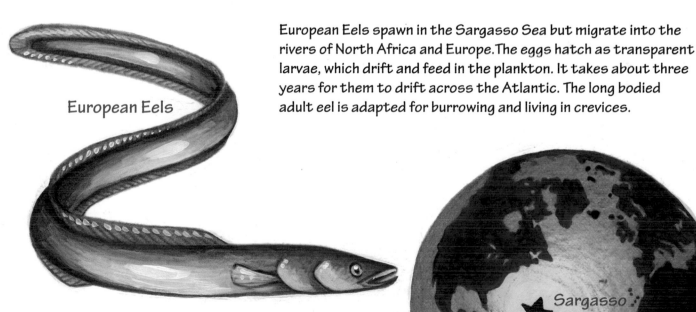

Salmon nest and spawn in rivers but migrate to sea to feed. Eggs hatch in the spring and young fish remain in the river, feeding on invertebrates usually for two to four years. Such a lifestyle is called anadromous. When about 15 cm long they migrate to the sea. In the sea, young salmon feed on shrimps and small fish. They grow rapidly. One to four years later, they return to the river to spawn. Salmon spawn in a nest (a "redd") dug into the gravel of the river bed.

Salmon

European Eels spawn in the Sargasso Sea but migrate into the rivers of North Africa and Europe. The eggs hatch as transparent larvae, which drift and feed in the plankton. It takes about three years for them to drift across the Atlantic. The long bodied adult eel is adapted for burrowing and living in crevices.

European Eels

Sargasso Sea

By traveling through underground streams, and even for short distances overland, eels sometimes reach ponds with no apparent direct connection to the sea.

Species which spawn at sea but migrate to freshwater are called catadromous.

Female eels may live twenty or more years in freshwater— males about six years.

What is a Fish?

Fins **Backbone**

Fins **Gills**

A fish is a backboned animal (a vertebrate) which lives in water throughout its life, has fins, and breathes by means of gills.

Gills are organs by which fish get oxygen from the water and also get rid of carbon dioxide.

Although all fish share these general features, they are not all closely related. In fact, the fish that live today are of four different major kinds (classes). Their internal structure shows that the four classes are distantly related but that they have followed different evolutionary paths. The "backbone" in many species is made of cartilage and not bone.

Pufferfish

Internal Structure

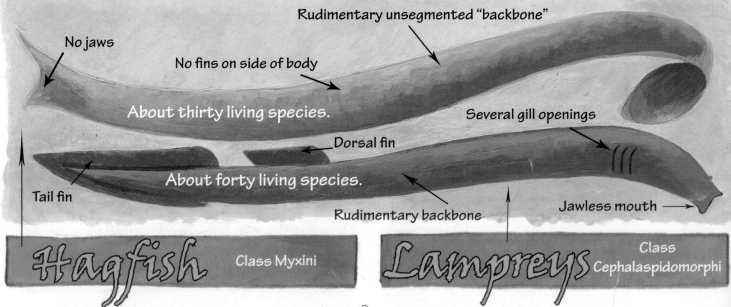

Rudimentary unsegmented "backbone"

No jaws

No fins on side of body

About thirty living species.

Several gill openings

Dorsal fin

About forty living species.

Tail fin

Rudimentary backbone

Jawless mouth

Hagfish Class Myxini

Lampreys Class Cephalaspidomorphi

Cartilaginous Fish

Class Chondrichthyes

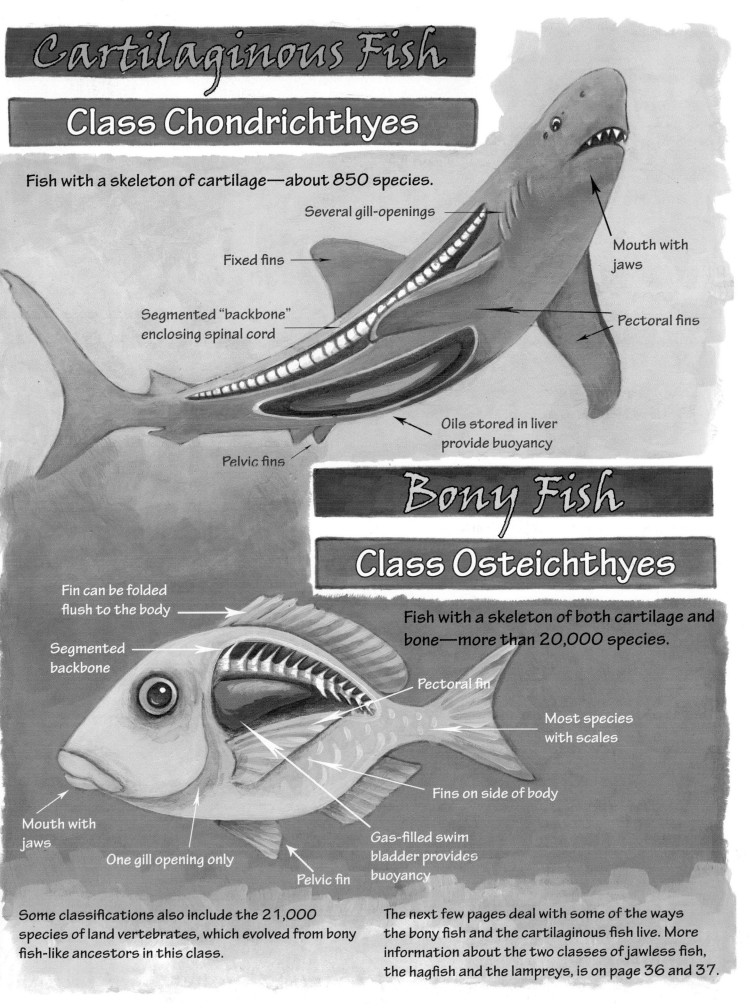

Fish with a skeleton of cartilage—about 850 species.

Several gill-openings

Fixed fins

Segmented "backbone" enclosing spinal cord

Mouth with jaws

Pectoral fins

Oils stored in liver provide buoyancy

Pelvic fins

Bony Fish

Class Osteichthyes

Fish with a skeleton of both cartilage and bone—more than 20,000 species.

Fin can be folded flush to the body

Segmented backbone

Pectoral fin

Most species with scales

Fins on side of body

Mouth with jaws

One gill opening only

Gas-filled swim bladder provides buoyancy

Pelvic fin

Some classifications also include the 21,000 species of land vertebrates, which evolved from bony fish-like ancestors in this class.

The next few pages deal with some of the ways the bony fish and the cartilaginous fish live. More information about the two classes of jawless fish, the hagfish and the lampreys, is on page 36 and 37.

What is Not a Fish?

Dispelling some misconceptions

There are several kinds of creatures that some people mistakenly call fish. Whales, dolphins, and porpoises are not fish.

They are mammals like ourselves. They breathe air and must surface to empty and refill their lungs. Their body shapes resemble those of fish, because streamlined shapes move most easily through water.

Dolphin

Tail beats up and down—not side to side as in most fish.

Porpoise

Nostrils on top of head breathe air.

Whale

Tadpoles are not fish. They are the larvae of amphibians (frogs, toads, newts, etc.). As larvae, amphibians have gills and live in water, but the adults of most species live on land and breathe air using lungs.

Jellyfish are not fish . . . nor are starfish— neither have a backbone or gills.

Octopus

Cuttlefish

Squids, octopus, and cuttlefish are not fish. They are mollusks, like slugs and snails. They have no backbone (invertebrates). Marine mollusks, together with some other invertebrates such as crustaceans (lobsters, crabs, shrimps, and prawns), are sometimes called "shellfish."

Lobsters, crabs, and crawfish are not fish . They are crustaceans. They live in water and breathe with gills, but have no backbone or fins.

Forward Power...

Most fish swim with a side to side movement. Contractions of large muscle blocks on either side of the fish make its body bend.

These muscle blocks are the fillets bought at the market. The fillets are made up of segments.

The fish's muscles are of two kinds—dark (red muscle) and light (white muscle). The two can be seen most easily in a fish steak. For normal swimming only, the red muscle is used. The white muscle is just for rapid bursts of speed.

Each segment contracts a fraction of a second later than the one in front, so that a wave of contraction passes along the fish. As a segment contracts, its partner on the other side of the fish is relaxed. The body is thrown into waves, which push outwards and backwards against the water, forcing the fish forward.

Most fish are stream-lined. They have tapering bodies which pass easily through water causing little disturbance, and so, little drag. High speed cruisers, such as mackerel, have more red muscle than less active fish, such as cod.

The Role of Fins

Fins enable fish to control their movements.

The caudal, or tail fin, has a large surface to push against the water and provides much of the forward power.

Dorsal and anal fins act as keels, preventing the fish from rolling.

The pectoral and pelvic fins act as stabilizers and also control rolling.

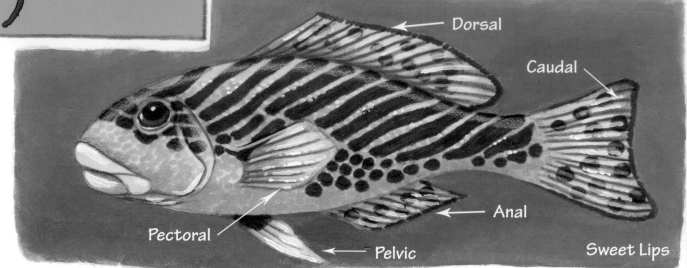

Dorsal

Caudal

Pectoral

Pelvic

Anal

Sweet Lips

Only the bony and cartilaginous fish have pectoral and pelvic fins. Lampreys and hagfish don't have them. The pectoral and pelvic fins control pitch, too.

In bony fish they can be unfurled to act as brakes and used as paddles for low speed swimming or for "treading water."

Fins of different shapes have evolved to suit different lifestyles.

Rolling

Pitch

An aircraft designed for high speed cruising.

Tail fins of fast-swimming fish are "v" shaped like wings of fast aircrafts to produce less drag.

The sailfish, the world's fastest swimming fish, is adapted for sustained high speed—Top speed over 45 mph (about 70 kmh).

Sailfish

But swept back fins (or wings) are less efficient for low speeds or maneuvering.

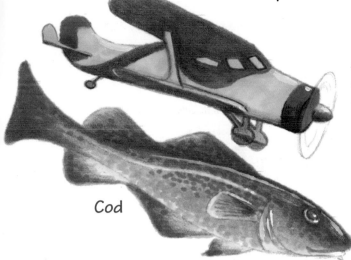

An aircraft built for aerobatics, its broad, stubby wings make it very maneuverable, but it can't fly fast.

Cod

Broad flat fins, like those of the cod family, give good maneuverability—but the cod isn't a very fast swimmer. Its top speed is about 15 mph (20 kmh).

Lurking predators, such as pike, which lunge at prey, have a dart-shaped body with fins set well back—A good arrangement for rapid acceleration from a standing start.

Pike

Different Strokes

Although most fish swim with a side to side motion, some species have other ways of getting about. . .

In rays, waves pass along the pectoral fins. The waves move up and down rather than side to side as in most fish.

Ray

Parrotfish keep their body rigid and row themselves along using their pectoral fins.

Parrotfish

13

Seahorse

Gurnards creep over the sea bed using the front three rays of each pectoral fin as delicate feelers.

Gurnard

Seahorses are among the slowest swimmers. They swim upright in the water using their dorsal fin to push themselves along. The tail is prehensile and can grasp objects so as to anchor the seahorse in favorable feeding sites. Slow swimmers like the seahorse are armored to protect them from predators.

Cowfish have the whole body, except the fins and mouth, encased in a bony box. They are slow and ungainly but well protected from predators.

Cowfish

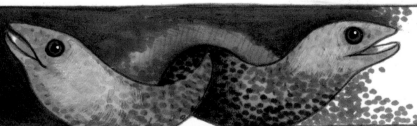

Eel

Other species, such as the eels, have evolved elongate shapes so that they can burrow or live in holes.

Hitching a Lift

Suckerfish

Suckerfish usually swim alongside their host, attaching to it only when it quickly changes speed or direction. They feed on crustaceans, including species which parasitize their hosts.

Flying fish, fast-swimming fish which live near the sea's surface, evade predators by leaping out of the water and gliding through the air on wing-like pectoral fins.

Flying Fish

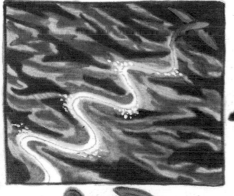

Hatchetfish

Freshwater hatchetfish have evolved powered flight. Beating their pectoral fins so fast they actually make a buzzing sound, they can fly through the air for short distances.

Pectoral fin   Flounder

Anal fin

Flat Fish

Both the bony and cartilaginous fish have evolved species with flattened bodies adapted for life on the seabed. The flat bony fish are flattened from side to side. As adults they lie on their sides. As the young fish develops, one eye moves over the skull so that in the adult fish both eyes are on the same side of the head.

Flattened cartilaginous fish are flattened from top to bottom.

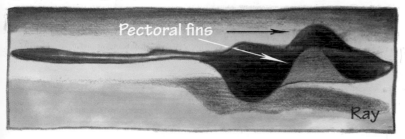

Pectoral fins

Ray

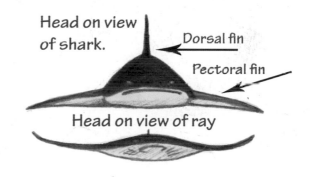

Head on view of shark.

Dorsal fin

Pectoral fin

Head on view of ray

The Next Generation

Some species produce lots of tiny eggs...

Each egg contains only a small food reserve (yolk) and must hatch once this is used up. They hatch into tiny larvae.

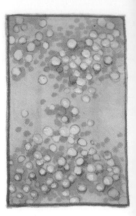

Egg production

Other species produce fewer, larger eggs. Each has a lot of yolk and the young fish develops to a larger size before hatching out.

Some small egg layers produce enormous numbers of eggs. A female cod may lay up to 6 million eggs in each season.

Cod

Ling

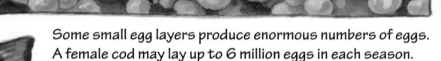

Ocean Sunfish

A large female ling can lay nearly 30 million eggs each year.

The ocean sunfish lays the most eggs—up to 300 million or more at a time. Whether eggs are large or small, within a species big fish produce more eggs than smaller fish produce. The eggs of any one species are all roughly the same size.

Protecting the young

Most fish shed their eggs into the water, there to be fertilized by sperm produced by the male.

Neither sperm nor unfertilized eggs survive long in water, so it's important that males and females are both ready at the same time.

Courtship has evolved to ensure they both shed at precisely the right moment.

16

The courtship of haddock, for example, involves special swimming movements.

The male develops a special spawning pattern and signals to the female with sounds which he produces by drumming with his swim bladder.

In haddock and other species which produce a lot of small eggs, once the eggs are fertilized they are abandoned by the parents.

Those fish which lay larger eggs have more invested in each. These species have evolved behaviors to protect their investment. Some build nests. . .

Trout

Coho Salmon

Salmon and trout dig nests in the riverbed. The female digs using her tail to produce an up current, which lifts gravel off the riverbed to be carried downstream by the current. Once the nest or "redd" is complete, the male and female lie close together. Stimulated by the presence of the male, the female lays her eggs. As she does so, the male fertilizes them. The female covers over the eggs with gravel, then abandons them. Protected beneath the gravel the eggs develop.

Stickleback

Other fish guard their nests.

Some gouramis build bubble nests of saliva blown by the male. Here he fiercely defends the developing eggs.

Gouramis

Sticklebacks lay their eggs in a nest, usually made from plant stems. When not chasing off potential predators, the male stands guard at the nest, fanning water over the eggs.

Some bony fish species protect their fertilized eggs and developing young by carrying them about. . .

Cowfish

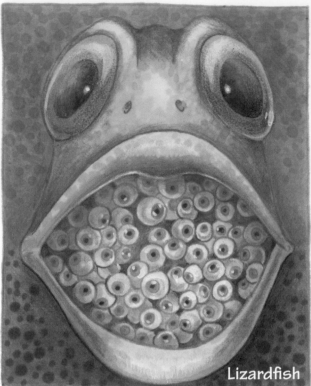

Lizardfish

Several species carry their offspring in their mouths. The breathing movements of the parent ensure that there is a good flow of oxygenated water over the eggs and young, but the parent can't feed whilst brooding.

Female sea horses lay their eggs in a brood pouch on the body of the male.

After two to six weeks the eggs have developed into tiny sea horses and are released from the pouch—it seems as if the male is giving birth.

Surf Perch

Some fish do not lay eggs at all. Instead they give birth to live young (they are viviparous). The eggs are fertilized inside the female and develop within her body. She gives birth to young which are miniature versions of the adult.

In some species the eggs are simply retained until they hatch, the developing embryos nourished by the yolk within the eggs—ovoviviparity.

Platies

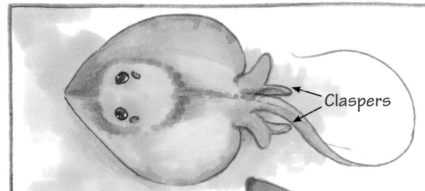
Claspers

In other species, the young are nourished from the mother's blood supply by a placenta-like structure—viviparity.

All cartilaginous fish have internal fertilization.

Males have claspers, with which they place sperm into the female.

Developing young

Many species of cartilaginous fish produce live young (either by ovoviviparity or viviparity)—but some lay eggs.

The egg is protected by an armored case laid down after the egg is fertilized, but before it is hatched.

Empty egg cases often wash ashore. They are sometimes called "mermaids' purses."

Most young fish die, either eaten by other fish or falling victim to other predators.

From all the eggs produced by each female, whether millions or just a few produced each season, on average only two will survive to spawn.

Egg case →

Yolk (food supply for developing young fish)

Tendrils to anchor egg to sea bed

Male or Female?

In most fish species, individuals are either one sex or the other, and remain so throughout their lives.

In cartilaginous fish, males can easily be distinguished from females by the presence of claspers.

Claspers are used by the male to place sperm inside the female.

Claspers

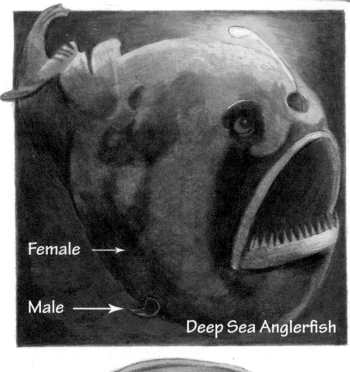

Female →

Male →

Deep Sea Anglerfish

In many bony fish it is difficult to tell the sexes apart.

But in some species, they look very different. Extreme examples are deep sea anglerfish.

Male anglerfish are small and live almost as parasites on the females. When a male finds a female, he bites on to her. The flesh of the male and female gradually fuses and he becomes permanently attached: available to fertilize eggs as required. The male is unable to catch food for himself and is nourished from the female.

Creole Wrasse

Indigo Hamlet

In some species, one individual may be both sexes—hermaphrodite.

A few fishes are both sexes at once—synchronous hermaphrodites.

Bass

Some species of bass are synchronous hermaphrodites—they spawn by trading eggs and sperm.

Goliath Grouper

Other species begin life as one sex, but as they grow, they change to the other sex—they are successive hermaphrodites.

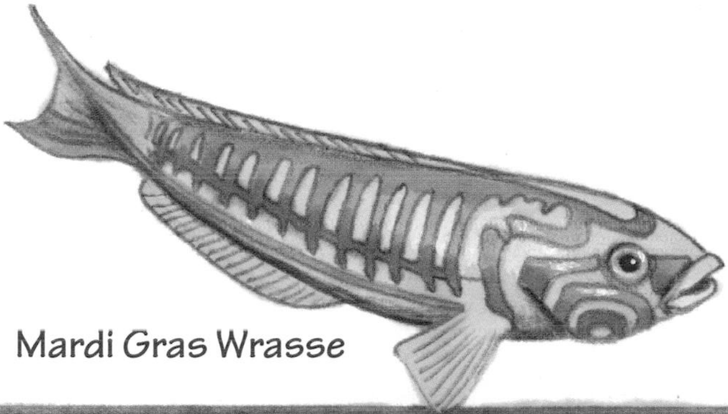

Mardi Gras Wrasse

In some species, individuals begin life as females but become males later on. This type of life history is most usually found in species such as some wrasse, in which a male controls a territory or harem. These dominant males began life as females. In other species, individuals begin life as males, becoming females as they grow.

Male to female changes occur in some deep-sea species which do not hold territories and in those species, such as anemone fish, in which a female controls the territory and dominates a group of males.

Clownfish

21

In a few species, there are several kinds of males. Atlantic salmon have two kinds. Males which have returned from the sea are big and have an upturned jaw with teeth developed for fighting. Males which have not yet been to sea are too small to fight a big male successfully or to court a female, but they can sneak into the nest and fertilize some of the eggs. In salmon the small males may later go to sea and grow up to be big males.

But in North American freshwater sunfish there are three kinds of males.

Large nesting males—the only kind to court a female. . .
Small sneaker males—who sneak into the nest whilst the nesting male is off guard.

Female impersonators mimic a female so they are tolerated in the nest by other males. Sneaker males and female impersonators never grow into large nest-building males.

Food for Fish

Fish have evolved to exploit a range of food items—almost everything from bacteria to mammals (including, occasionally, people).

Except for the hagfish and lampreys (see page 8), all living vertebrates have jaws.

Jaws evolved from the part of the skeleton that supports the gills.

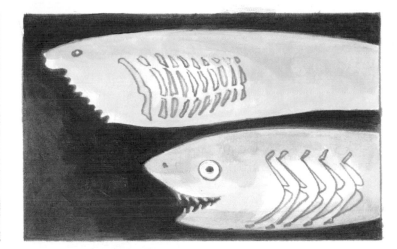

During the course of evolution, the front supports have swung forward to lie above and below the mouth and have become hinged.

Powerful muscles evolved to slam the lower jaw upwards against the upper, and the jaws became armed with teeth.

In the cartilaginous fish, only the upper and lower jaws have teeth, but in bony fish other bones of the head have become modified to form part of the bite, and teeth may occur on the tongue, the insides of the cheeks, and the roof of the mouth. The evolution of jaws and teeth allowed fish to eat many different kinds of food.

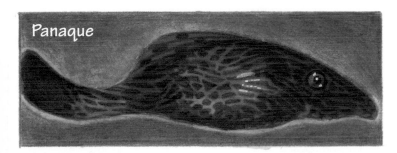

Panaque

All the cartilaginous fish are carnivores (flesh eaters). But among bony fish are both herbivores (plant eaters) and carnivores—and some which eat both plants and animals (omnivores).

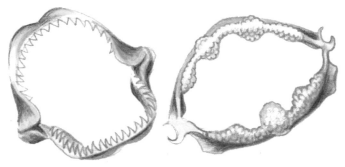

Teeth have become adapted to deal with different types of food. Predatory sharks have sharp serrated teeth, like steak knives, for slicing through flesh. Shellfish feeders have stout, flattened teeth with which to crack open the hard bodies of their prey.

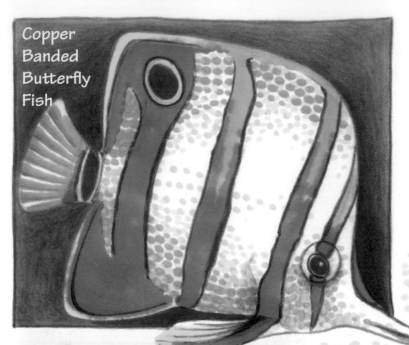

Copper Banded Butterfly Fish

The shape of the mouth has also evolved to allow different feeding styles— here are just a few examples.

Butterfly fish have long jaws for picking prey from crevices.

The upturned mouth of ricefish is adapted for taking insects from the water's surface.

Ricefish

The earliest jaws to evolve were used simply to grasp prey.

Sucker Fish

The underslung mouth of a sucker is adapted for feeding on the bottom.

But many species have evolved more mobile jaws adapted for sucking prey into the mouth.

As the fish approaches food, it extends its mouth forward to form a narrow tube—rapid expansion of the inside of the mouth sucks in the prey.

Grouper

Some large predatory sharks, such as the great white shark, have evolved an unusual style of feeding—taking chunks out of prey too large to be swallowed whole.

As the mouth opens to bite, the upper jaw rolls forward.

Great White Shark

These sharks feed mainly on seals and sea lions. Sometimes they attack swimmers, possibly mistaking them for seals, but shark attacks on people are rare—worldwide, sharks attack fewer than one hundred people a year.

Goldfish

Some fish only have tiny teeth in the jaws or none at all. Fish of the carp family, for example the goldfish, have grinding teeth in the throat—possibly an adaptation to squeeze water from the food before it is swallowed.

Others have evolved specialized structures on the gill used to filter their food from the water.

In most fish, gill rakers act as a screen, preventing debris being flushed over delicate gills.

Gill rakers

Sieve

Gills

But in some species, rakers are modified into a fine comb, which filters small items from the water as it passes in through the mouth and out over the gills. Particles sieved out collect at the back of the mouth and are swallowed as food.

This is an efficient way of gathering food. The world's two largest fish, the whale shark and the basking shark, feed by filtering small animals from the water. The teeth of these sharks are tiny and not used in feeding.

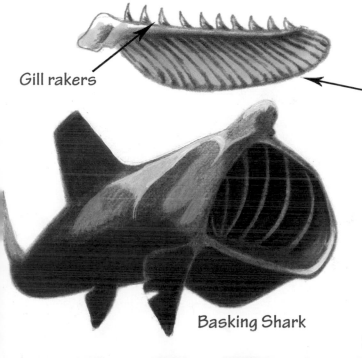

Basking Shark

25

Food for Thought

"Older than agriculture, the history of fishing. . .is as old as mankind." — Prof. Andres von Brandt

Even our pre-human ancestors may have hunted freshwater fish.

In the Olduvai Gorge, Tanzania, fish bones have been found associated with pre-human remains dating back nearly two million years.

Fish are the only wild animals still extensively hunted in the developed world.

As technology developed, humans became predators, not only of freshwater fish, but also of sea fish.

Hunting of wild stocks, at a sustainable level, has far less impact on the environment than does agriculture.

Controlled fishing is an environmentally friendly way for us to obtain food, and it is extremely good food, rich in protein, vitamins, and minerals—yet low in fat.

Olduvai Gorge, Tanzania

In most fish, the power for swimming is generated in large muscles on either side of the body. These muscles are what we eat as fish flesh. A large amount of muscle is needed to propel a fish—it takes a lot of power to push water aside. In most fish, more than half the body weight is muscle.

Fish contain relatively little fat and much of what they do contain is unsaturated. Recent research shows that eating only fish (such as herring and mackerel) can reduce our risk of heart disease. Only fish contain certain fatty acids which help prevent our blood vessels clogging with cholesterol.

Certain oils contained in fish also appear to be essential for normal brain development. "Fish is good brain food" isn't just an old wives' tale.

Fish are also rich in vitamins and minerals. Their oils contain especially large amounts.

Drinking fish oil is one way to get these constituents which are vital for our health.

But including fish, especially oily fish, as a part of the diet is a more pleasant means of ensuring we get the vitamins and minerals we need.

So eating fish is good for our health—and not bad for the health of the planet. Managed with care, fish stocks can be harvested as a renewable resource, with little damage to the environment.

Provided we regulate fishing so that stocks are not overfished and ensure that our rivers, lakes, and seas do not become poisoned by pollution, we can all go on enjoying the rich variety of fish, maybe for another two million years or longer.

Do Fish Drink?

Some do

Some don't

Generally, fish in the sea drink a lot.

Those in freshwater drink very little.

The reason—if two solutions are separated by a membrane, water flows from the more dilute to the more concentrated solution—a process called osmosis. A semi-permeable membrane allows water but not salts to pass through.

Osmosis

Fish skin is fairly waterproof, but delicate surfaces, such as the gills, act as semi-permeable membranes separating the fish's blood from the surrounding water.

Blood carries essential salts around the body, but the blood is less salty than sea water and a fish in the sea is constantly losing water by osmosis.

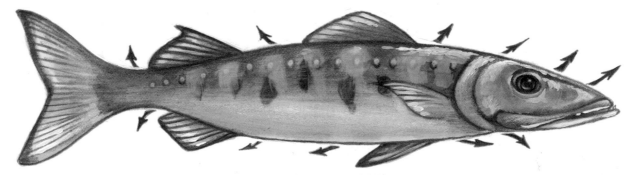

Marine fish make good this water loss by drinking lots of sea water. The extra salt consumed is pumped out of the body by special cells on the gills.

In freshwater the opposite is true; the fish blood is more salty than freshwater and water is driven into the fish by osmosis.

Freshwater fish drink as little as possible.

Excess water swallowed with food or driven into the fish by osmosis is excreted as dilute urine. Salt is actively pumped into the fish by special cells on the gills.

Damage to the skin of fish makes them leak, causing them great stress in dealing with the loss or gain of water or salts, as well as providing a site for infection.

Always handle fish carefully! And never with dry hands.

The skin of a bony fish is very delicate and covers the scales .

Loss of scales indicates a major loss of skin—a wound equivalent to a burn in humans.

Freshwater Sunfish

Scale embedded in skin

Baby Sand Shark

Cartilaginous fish drink less than bony fish.

Cownose Ray

Concentrated salts and urea.

By storing urea in the blood, they raise its concentration to that of the surrounding seawater.

Urea is a by-product of life processes in animals. It is very toxic to most animals, and they keep its concentration in their blood low by passing it out in the urine. The tissues of sharks and rays are more tolerant of urea than are those of most animals. Sharks and rays that have been dead for some hours have an unpleasant smell as the urea breaks down into ammonia.

Colors and Camouflage

Cardinal Fish

For any animal, colors and patterns are a trade-off. Bright colors and vivid pattern may help to make an animal conspicuous and recognizable to a mate, but they also make it obvious to potential prey and to predators.

Striking colors and patterns have evolved particularly in environments where there are many species living side by side (e.g. coral reefs)...

Moorish Idols

...perhaps recognizing and being recognized by one's own species is especially important here.

Some very showy patterns have evolved as warnings to potential predators that a species is too spiny or too poisonous to be worth pursuing.

In some surgeon fish, bands of color highlight the blade-like spines on the tail and may warn off predators.

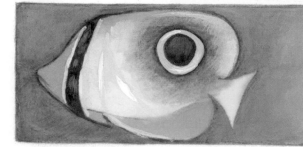

Surgeon Fish

The red and black color of the lionfish warns of highly venomous tips to the fins.

Lionfish

Patterns are sometimes misleading—eye spot makes this look like the mouth of a big fish. The real eye is disguised by a black band.

Eye spots, like those of butterflyfish, may have evolved to trick predators into misdirecting attacks or believing a fish is bigger and more ferocious than it really is.

Jacks

Silvering also provides camouflage. The gleaming flank of the fish is like a mirror and difficult to see underwater.

Shape is another aid to blending in with the background.

Angelfish

Some fish, which normally are camouflaged, develop bright colors or patterns in the breeding season.

Becoming more obvious to predators is outweighed by the better chance of attracting a mate.

Pipefish are difficult to distinguish from the weed in which they hunt.

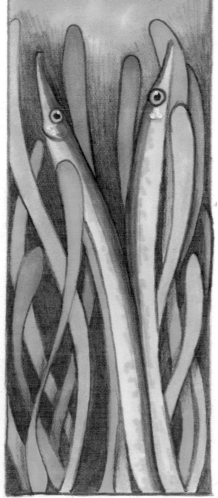

At spawning time, the normally drab male stickleback becomes very conspicuous.

Countershading

Patterns may disguise the outline of a fish. One pattern found on nearly all fish is countershading: darkly pigmented above, light colored below. Countershading works like this—a body lit from above would normally have its lower half in shadow. The dark upper part blends in with the shadowed underside so that the outline of the body does not show up against the background.

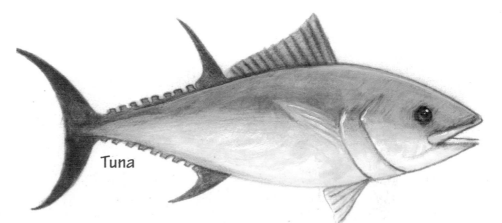

Tuna

Countershading also means that when viewed from above, the dark upper surface of the fish is difficult to see against the dark background of water. Viewed from below, the light underbelly is difficult to see against the light surface.

Tricks of the Light

Midshipman

In the deep sea, there is not enough light for normal countershading to be effective. Deep sea fish have evolved a special kind of camouflage which involves them producing their own light. To a predator viewing it from below, a fish would normally appear as a dark silhouette against the background light filtering down from the surface.

Midshipman seen from below

So, many deep sea fish have evolved light organs which produce a downward directed light of similar brightness and color to the background illumination. With its lights on, the fish in effect disappears into the background.

Light organs can produce only a dim light, so light camouflage systems have evolved only in the deep sea where background light-levels are low. In the twilight world of the deep ocean, lights also serve as signals. The arrangement of lights on the bodies of some fish allows them to recognize others of their own species and even tell the individuals' sex.

Midshipman light display from the side

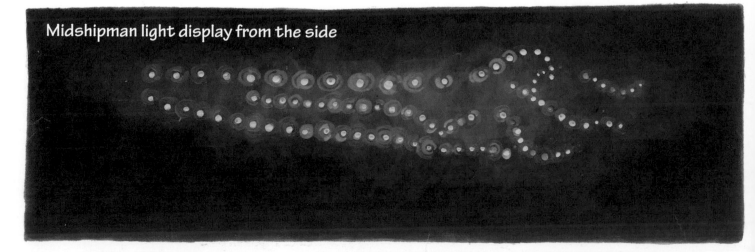

Electricity

A SUPERSENSE

All animals work by electricity—the tiny electrical currents which flow along nerves and cause muscles to contract.

Sharks have evolved sensors that allow them to locate their prey by detecting the electrical current it produces.

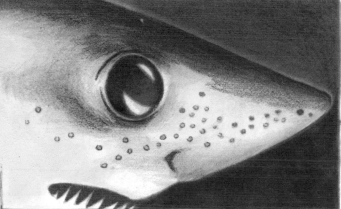

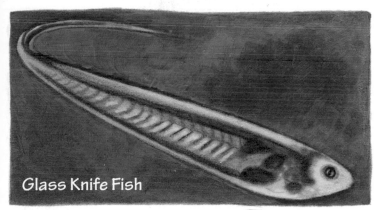

Glass Knife Fish

Other fish use electric fields as a sort of radar. Using specialized electricity producing organs, made up of modified muscles, the fish surrounds itself with an electric field.

A series of special sense organs along the side of the fish detects distortions of this weak field caused by nearby objects or the presence of other fish.

In this way, the fish builds up an electrical image of its surroundings. Most weakly electric fish are either nocturnal or live in murky waters: this electrical "view" of their environment is vital to them in finding food and avoiding obstacles and predators.

Through discharges of their electric organs they can also communicate with others of their own species.

Bulls Eye Guitarfish

And a SUPERWEAPON

In several species the ability to produce electricity has developed even further. These fish have large electric organs, occupying up to one third of the body's bulk. They produce not only weak electric fields, by which they navigate and find prey, but also massive electric shocks that are used to deter predators and stun prey.

The electric eel from the rivers of tropical South America can produce up to 650 volts, and the electric ray found in British waters can generate 220 volts.

Vertebrate Relations

Fish *do* have features in common: they are backboned animals (vertebrates) which live in water throughout their lives, have fins, and breathe by means of gills.

But not all fish are closely related. To understand why, we need to look at the evolution of the vertebrates.

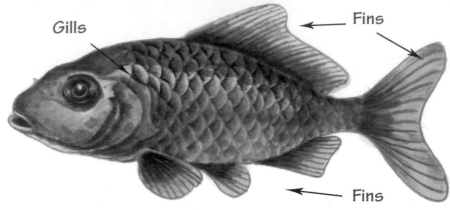

Gills

Fins

Fins

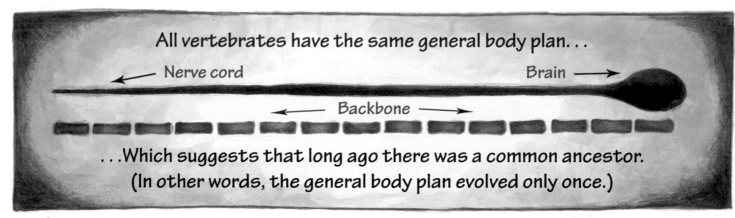

All vertebrates have the same general body plan. . .

Nerve cord

Brain

← Backbone →

. . .Which suggests that long ago there was a common ancestor.
(In other words, the general body plan evolved only once.)

However, from this common ancestor several different evolutionary pathways then followed.
The vertebrates alive today belong to four major groups (classes) which are only distantly related to one another.

All four groups contain animals that fit within our definition of fish but only one group, the bony vertebrates, also includes all the land living vertebrates—including ourselves.

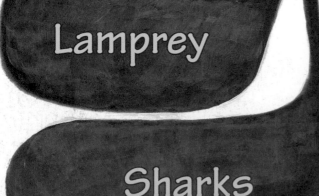

Lamprey

Hagfish

Sharks

Bony fish

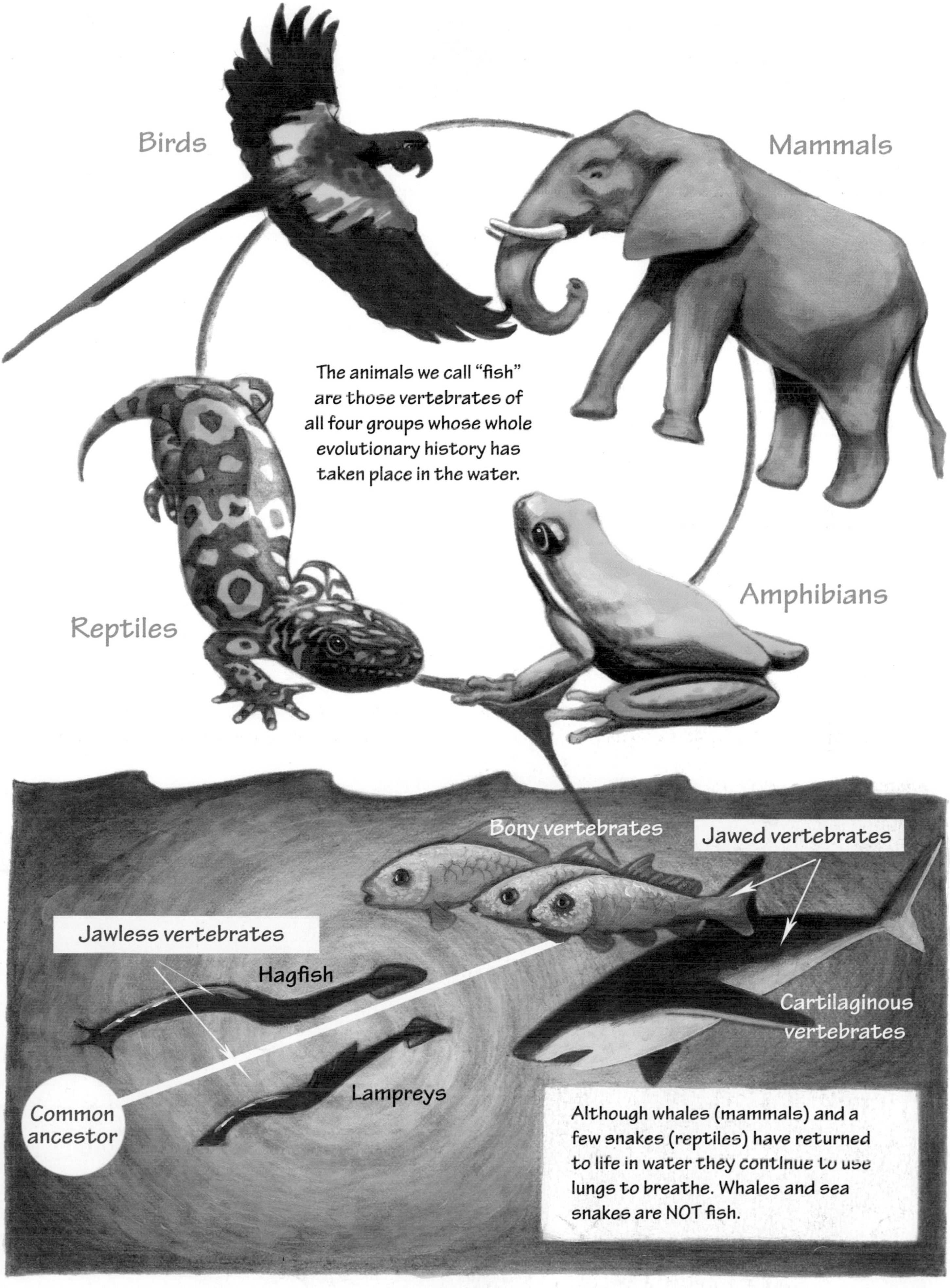

Birds

Mammals

The animals we call "fish" are those vertebrates of all four groups whose whole evolutionary history has taken place in the water.

Amphibians

Reptiles

Bony vertebrates

Jawed vertebrates

Jawless vertebrates

Hagfish

Cartilaginous vertebrates

Lampreys

Common ancestor

Although whales (mammals) and a few snakes (reptiles) have returned to life in water they continue to use lungs to breathe. Whales and sea snakes are NOT fish.

Before they evolved jaws, vertebrates were all filter feeders or scavengers and were limited to small, immobile, or soft-bodied prey.

Most jawless forms are now extinct. We know them only from their fossils.

Only two kinds survived to evolve to the present day—hagfish and lampreys.

The Jawless Ones

Neither closely resembles their jawless ancestors, for they have evolved specialist ways of life. Only by this have they been able to compete successfully with jawed fish.

HAGFISH—Class Myxini

Hagfish are blind, elongate creatures that look so wormlike they were for a time thought to be worms. But their internal structure shows them to be closely related to the other vertebrates. They produce foul but useful slime and tie themselves in knots.

They look wormlike because they have evolved a wormlike way of life, burrowing in the marine mud, hunting worms and shrimps.

They even have wormlike mouths with toothed horny plates on either side of the mouth. These bite with a side to side action (in true jaws the lower bites against the upper).

Hagfish are not only predators but also scavengers. They burrow into dead and dying fish and eat them from the inside.

They can be a serious pest of some fisheries.

More than one hundred hagfish have been taken from a single fish carcass.

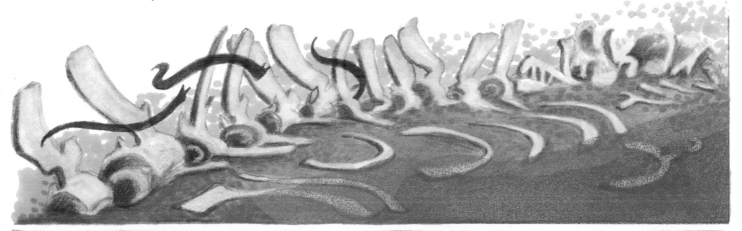

LAMPREYS—Class Cephalaspidomorphi

Larval Lampreys—Ammocoetes—live in the mud of rivers.
They feed by filtering microscopic plants from the mud surface.

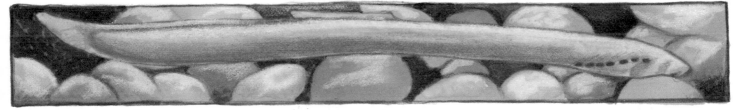

In most species the larval phase lasts three to eight years. As they change into the adult form, lampreys develop eyes and a round sucker-like mouth armed with horny teeth. The sucker-like mouth is used to move stones from the stream bed to make a saucer-shaped nest. Only about half of the forty-one species of lamprey feed as adults. The rest spawn soon after becoming adult. Those that do feed are blood suckers. The lamprey clamps on to its victim and uses its tongue to rasp a hole. It drinks the blood and tissue debris that flows from the wound—an anti-coagulant in the saliva ensures a steady flow of blood.

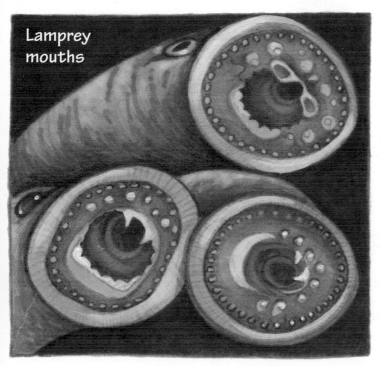

Lamprey mouths

Salmon with Lampreys

All lampreys spawn and spend their larval life in freshwater, but adults of some species migrate to sea where they attach to a variety of different fish. All species spawn only once. The adults die soon after spawning.

Bony Ones—Class Osteichthyes

These vertebrates have a skeleton of both cartilage and bone. Their body plan has enabled them to adapt to many different environments. Today there are more than 40,000 species—but only about half of them are fish.

Some 370 million years ago, some bony vertebrates evolved ways of living out of water. They became the land animals, tetrapods (tetrapod = four feet).

There are today about 21,000 species of tetrapod: mammals (including us), amphibians, birds, and reptiles. Those that remained in the waters have evolved into present-day bony fish.

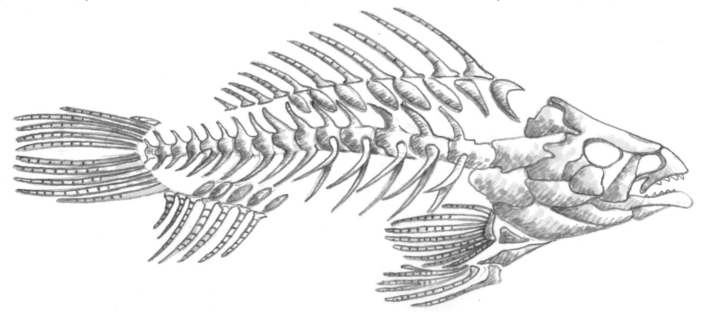

Through details of their skeleton, they can be divided into four sub-classes. Three of the sub-classes are small, containing only eighteen species between them. The fourth, the ray-finned bony fish, is the most successful, with more than 20,000 species alive today.

LUNGFISH
Sub Class Dipneusti

There are only six living species: one in Australia, one in South America, and four in Africa. All live in freshwater.

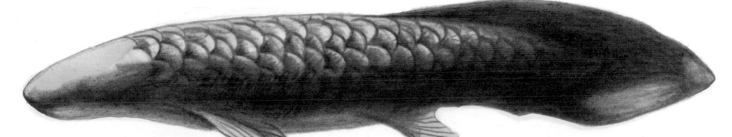

In stagnant, poorly oxygenated water, these fish switch to breathing air, using their large swim bladder as a lung. Some African lungfish species can survive even when their pond dries up completely. As the water level falls, they burrow into the muddy bottom and secrete a cocoon of mucus. The fish remains dormant until the pond refills. Becoming dormant during hot or dry periods is called estivation.

Many species of coelacanth, nearly all freshwater, are known from fossils. . .

COELACANTH
Sub Class Crossopterygii

. . .But this sub class was thought to have become extinct along with the dinosaurs until 1938, when one was caught in the sea off South Africa. Since then over one hundred specimens have been caught, all but the first one, off the Comoro Islands in the Pacific Ocean.

BICHIRS
Sub Class Brachiopterygii

These fish have well developed swim bladders, and in poorly oxygenated water they can use them to breathe air. There are only eleven species—all live in freshwaters of tropical Africa.

RAY-FINNED BONY FISH
Sub Class Actinopterygii

The success story of modern fish: they have evolved to live in nearly all the waters of the earth and there are more than 20,000 species.

Chondrostei—Sturgeons and Paddlefish (Twenty-five species)

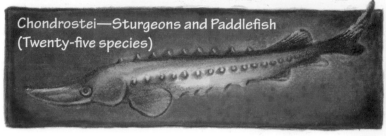

Lepisosteiformes—Gars (Seven species)

There are three very small and one very large group of ray-finned bony fish. . .

Sturgeons and paddlefish, gars, and bowfin are living remnants of kinds of ray-finned fish, which, once plentiful, have largely been replaced by the enormously successful Teleostei.

Amiiformes—Bowfin (One species)

TELEOSTEI

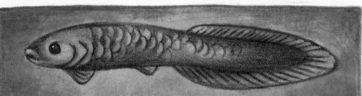

Elopomorpha—Eels and relatives—adults don't look alike, but all have similar transparent leaf-shaped larva. All spawn at sea; some enter freshwater to feed. (About 630 Species)

Osteoglossomorpha—Bony tongues—The bite is mainly teeth or tongue pressing up against teeth on roof of mouth. All live in freshwater. (About 116 species)

Ostariophysi—Carp, Tetras, Catfish, and relatives—The dominant group in freshwater—only a few live in the sea. If alarmed or injured, most species secrete a special chemical which alerts other fish to danger. Specially adapted bones transmit vibrations from the swim bladder to the head giving these fish exceptional hearing. (About 6,050 species)

Clupeomorpha—Herring, Anchovies, and relatives—Canals connect swim bladders with ears, giving fish acute hearing. There is also a connection between the swim bladder and gut. Most are marine. (About 340 Species)

Protacanthopterygii—Pike, Salmon, and relatives—Most marine fish which enter fresh water belong to this group. (About 300 species.)

Flashlight Fish

Scopelomorpha—Lizardfish, Lanternfish, and relatives—mainly deep sea fish—some have light organs. (About 440 species.)

Acanthopterygii—Silversides and Spiny-finned fish. Largest super-order of living fish. Most have sharp spines in dorsal and anal fins. In many, pelvic fin is beneath pectoral fin. (About 11,500 species)

Talapia

Cod

Hatchetfish

Paracanthopterygii—Cod, Anglerfish, and relatives—Mostly marine fish in which the pelvic fin is forward on the body, usually beneath the pectoral fin. The dorsal and anal fins are supported by rays, not spines. (About 1,160 species)

Stenopterygii—Bristlemouths, Hatchetfish, and relatives. (About 250 Species)

The Gristly Ones

These vertebrates have evolved a skeleton of cartilage—a gristle-like material which is light yet strong. These fish are of two main kinds:

Sub Class Holocephali (Thirty species)

Sub Class Elasmobranchii (About 850 Species)

Sub Class Holocephali (Thirty species)— Rabbitfish or Chimaera—A single gill-opening on either side. The Holocephali are all marine fish, usually living in cooler seas, some species at great depth.

Sub Class Elasmobranchii (About 850 Species)— Sharks and Rays—have multiple gill-openings (usually five, but six or seven in some species). In the seas, the Elasmobranchii have been very successful, but only as carnivores; these are no plant-eating species. Many are predators of bony fish. They are less suited than bony fish to life in freshwater (see page 28) and almost all live in the sea.

Classification of Elasmobranchii fish is based mainly upon characteristics of the head skeleton. They can be divided into thirteen kinds (orders).

Five of the orders contain flattened species in which both the mouth and the gill-openings are on the underside—these are the rays.

Nostrils

Mouth

Gill openings

The flattened body is an adaptation to life on the seabed. To overcome the problem of breathing whilst the mouth is in contact with the sea floor, the rays breathe in through the spiracle—a hole on either side of the head just behind the eye.

42

Guitar Fish—Order Rhinobatiformes—
Rays with a stout tail and large tail fin.
(About fifty species)

Electric Rays—Order Torpediniformes—Stout-
bodied rays which produce a powerful electric
shock (see page 33). (About forty-five species)

Sawfish—Order Pristiformes—Rays in
which the snout forms a saw-like blade. The
saw is used to dig crabs and other prey out
of the seabed. The sawfish also eats small
fish it kills by thrashing the saw from side
to side. (About seven species)

Typical Rays—
Order Rajiformes—
Bottom-living rays
with a disc-shaped
body and slender
tail. (About 220
species).

Sting Rays, Manta Rays,
and relatives—Order
Myliobatiformes—Rays with a
disc-shaped body and a very
slender tail, usually with a
venomous spine. (About 180
species) Manta Rays don't
have venomous spines.

Although most rays live on the seabed, some
Myliobatiformes have abandoned the sea floors
for a life near the surface. The Manta Ray, for
example, is a surface dweller. Its huge flattened
body acts as a parachute helping to prevent it
from sinking.

The other eight orders have their gill-openings on the side of the head—these are the sharks.

Spiny Sharks
Order Squaliformes

Spines

Spiny Dog-fish Shark

No anal fin

Sharks without an anal fin, but with two dorsal fins, usually with a stout spine in front of both. Most of the eighty species live near the seabed.

Saw Sharks
Order Squaliformes

Sharks with the snout projecting as a toothed blade. (Six species)

These sharks use the saw with a side to side thrashing action to disable the fish and squid on which they prey.

They resemble sawfish, but unlike them, their gill-openings are on the side of the head and there is a pair of sensory barbels on the saw.

Angel Sharks
Order Squaliformes

Flattened bottom-living sharks resemble rays but the large pectoral fins are not fused to the head as in rays. (About thirteen species).

Gill openings on the side of head

44

Port Jackson Sharks
Order Heterodontiformes

Stout bottom-living sharks with an anal fin and spines in front of both dorsal fins.

All live in tropical or sub-tropical seas. Unlike other living sharks, they have both pointed, grasping teeth and flattened, grinding teeth. (Eight species)

Port Jackson Shark

Six & Seven Gilled Sharks
Order Hexanchiformes

Sharks with an anal fin, a single dorsal fin, and six or seven gill openings, mainly in cooler, deep seas. (Five species)

Frilled Shark

Whale Shark

Carpet Sharks
Order Orectolobiformes

Sharks with two dorsal fins and an anal fin. Most species have barbels at the edges of the nostrils. Barbels are sensitive to food in the water.

Spotted Wobbegong

Many carpet sharks are sluggish bottom feeders, but the order also includes the largest of the world's fish, the huge filter-feeding whale shark. (About thirty-five species)

Mackerel Sharks
Order Lamniformes

Sharks with two dorsal fins, without spines, and an anal fin.

Most are fast, active predators, (such as the great white shark, the mako, and the porbeagle), adapted for fast cruising. But the order also contains two filter-feeders, the basking shark and the recently discovered megamouth. (About sixteen species)

Great White

Mako

Porbeagle

Megamouth

Ground Sharks
Order Carcharhiniformes

Most sharks belong to this order. It contains about two hundred species. Like Lamniform sharks, they have two dorsal fins and an anal fin. The Carcharhiniform sharks, however, have a moveable eyelid which protects the eye.

Eyelid or "nictitating" membrane

Dogfishes

Some, such as dogfishes, are sluggish bottom dwellers feeding mainly on invertebrates.

Blue Shark

Others, such as the blue shark, are large active oceanic predators.

Sharks of this order are very varied. The order also includes nine species of hammer-heads, sharks with flattened heads.

The flattened head may act as a wing giving extra lift and aiding maneuverability. Other theories suggest it evolved to provide a larger area for sense organs, and that having eyes widely separated gives the shark good stereoscopic vision.

Eyes

Questions?

Attention Seeking: Why attract attention?

Page 30

Brains: Why are fish good for them?

Page 27

Cruising: Which muscles are used?

Page 11

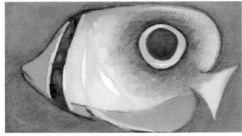

Eye Spots: Why do some fish have them?

Page 30

Flight: Which fish fly?

Page 15

Hermaphrodites: What are they?

Pages 20-21

Lights: What are they used for?

Page 32

Pipefish: How are they disguised?

Page 31

Vampires: Which fish drink blood?

Page 31